# RANKIN

## *v.*

# RANKIN

## A Father's Divorce and Custody Fight(s) within the Mississippi Judicial System

### KELVIN RANKIN

PAGE PUBLISHING
Conneaut Lake, PA

First originally published by Page Publishing 2024

ISBN 979-8-89157-221-8 (pbk)
ISBN 979-8-89157-225-6 (digital)

Printed in the United States of America

# INTRODUCTION

J ust because justice is evoked doesn't mean justice is always involved completely. It is important to convey background information for the reader to understand the purpose of this book. The aim is to give husbands and fathers hope by giving a glimpse into the chaos divorce brings to the family and himself as viewed from my experiences. "If" the male decides to forgo the status quo and challenge both a divorce and child custody to the mother, expect adjudication at times to fall into the "gray areas" of what would be considered justice. This dialogue encompasses actions in Chancery Courts, Youth Court, Court of Appeals, Supreme Court, interactions with law enforcement, Child Protective Services, and various other entities primarily in the state of Mississippi. Supreme Case Law No. 2019-CT-00238-SCT was the decisive decision whereby truth began to reign over perceptions manifested by the challenger (former spouse) and those in support of that failed endeavor.

Personally, as a person of conviction, marriage is a covenant. When the relationship failed, it became a legal contract needing adjudication. From 2017 to the present (2023), nothing has been more lethal to my emotional, physical, or psychological well-being. Having to face the interrogation of staring eyes from family, friends, associates, and folk in general with the thought of *He must have wronged her in some way* can weigh heavily on one's mind. From what seemed like a beautiful relationship to outsiders now evoked a very public fight that painted me as a man being guilty before innocence was proven. It's how our society is conditioned as related to divorce and child custody issues. Subjective observations indicate that more often, legal decisions of divorce and particularly child custody are more favorable to women.

A perfect depiction of a wrongly conceived perception was with my mentor and friend of whom we ate breakfast together routinely. As he observed every step of the process and before his untimely death in 2022, my friend asked me to forgive him because he thought I was the guilty party. He was forgiven, for by this time, I had come to terms with how one's perception can differ from reality. As with many, including my family, the initial impression was that I was at fault for the failure of a relationship and the woman should raise my children regardless and without a fight. Their advisement was to give her the divorce she wanted and move on. The perception did not work in my favor (in part) in that I am an Army Infantry Veteran, Airborne Ranger qualified, having commanded at one point a Ranger Training Company, six foot one, bass voice, and decisive with my actions. Some of these qualities and qualifications were used against me in one appellate court and public opinion. In stark contrast, there was no real consideration in my favor that I was an ordained pastor, seminary-trained, a public servant, and no civil or criminal record or suchlike. Overall I was viewed as guilty before having my day in court in the eyes of many.

At my very first court appearance (January 2018) in the Warren County Chancery Court, there were (as I recall) twenty cases before the chancellor, dealing with submitting pleas and deals on behalf of plaintiffs and defendants concerning divorce and custody. Eighteen of the twenty were no contests, of which (as I recall) the men did not bother to appear. As I appeared with my attorney, I declined to accept the plaintiff's deal of a divorce on irreconcilable differences or the surrendering of my parental rights. That resolute decision and the quest for the truth of the "why" of the divorce request and change in the paternal relationship had to be addressed to bring about a proper resolution. My decision drew a red line in the ensuing contestation.

By no means do I advocate that every relationship is worth saving, and in some situations, there is an inadequate parent (male or female), which warrants one parent over another having primary child custody. However, if you are a man of conviction, have done right by your family, and find yourself in the prementioned situation(s)…read on for support. I'll make this as simple as possible using my experience as a case study.

There are two critical points for the reader to understand. One, there are parts whereby the intricate details will not be shared primarily as it relates to issues with my children. If you decide to take the route less traveled by many men and contest a divorce or custody of children, you might be surprised by what you "did not know" that will shake you to your core. Second, this book is going to be one-sided throughout. There are two sides to every story, and this story is summarized in court decisions and (at present) ensuing nonrelated but qualitative litigation that will be used as part of the final custody status of the children. Trust me, I don't claim perfection. I claim that I am one who loved my spouse and children but had to choose between simply accepting a deal or taking the road less traveled.

# THE PROCLAMATION: "I WANT A DIVORCE!"

Most divorce requests don't simply appear. Prior to my former spouse soliciting a divorce, it was discussed, dismissed, brought back up again in conversation, and dealt with in multiple counseling sessions until that fateful day of her making that final proclamation: "*I want a divorce!*" The state of Mississippi gets criticism for its no-fault divorce law in that both the husband and wife must agree (of which I did not); unlike other states (except South Dakota), a spouse can get a divorce without the agreeance of the other. Every state has its own nuances by which one may get divorced. In Mississippi, if both do not agree to a divorce on irreconcilable differences or paternal custody, at a minimum, divorce must be adjudicated before final custody is decided. In theory, the division of marital assets and a host of other issues can be decided upon. Yet, in my case, everything was and in part still being contested before Chancery Court for a final order detailing the terms of custody. In a contested divorce on grounds, you're at the mercy of the court(s) to make a permanent and lasting decision affecting all within the fractured family unit.

In November 2017, my spouse moved out of the marital home under the guise that a temporary separation was what "we" needed. Prior to her moving out, the subject was broached with the suggestion that I should leave the home to maintain the stability of our children. *Let me be clear. Do not voluntarily leave your home attempting to be manly!* When I refused to leave, it was recommended that I help her move items into her apartment to allow the children to see that we were "okay" with the one-sided decision. *Let me be clear. Do not participate in activities that you are not in agreeance with*! I never moved one item from the marital home to her new place. As difficult as it was, I observed her packing and moving items all by herself using her sedan. True to the situation, what was being presented was the ploy to divorce. Amazingly enough, she assumed she would have physical custody of the children in that she expressed it would be best for the children. Why not. This is the perceived trend. *Let me be clear. Do not give up your parental rights under the rationale that the mother is better suited than you*! Acquaintances, family, and friends will begin making potentially unqualified judgment calls. *Let me be clear. Do not let your spouse's choices deter you from being visible in the community you live in. Just be as respectful as possible until you understand what changes to make relationally.*

In December 2017, I received a frantic call from my attorney to not communicate with my wife. She had filed for divorce on the grounds of "habitual cruel and inhuman treatment" and in the alternative "irreconcilable differences." The only thing that was missing was my being served divorce papers. I remember the night I was served. I arrived home late at night and was backing up into my driveway when a car came out of nowhere speeding, and out jumped a little thin lady handing me papers, saying I was served. "Kinda" out of a movie. At least I was not surprised. The paperwork gave the instructions, which I shared with my attorney the following day.

January 2018 was our first appearance in court, as mentioned in the introduction. Literally the morning of the scheduled hearing, I found myself along with my attorney in the office of the opposing attorney (at his invitation) of which a deal was presented—divorce on irreconcilable differences, parental visitation every other weekend, child support, and other nonnegotiables for me. I promptly declined and walked out. There was nothing to discuss. I needed answers before agreeing to anything. With the decision not to "play ball," this would begin the contestation that would expose the deepest of pillow talk. Nothing would be off-limits or considered sacred for open court discussions.

# REALITIES TO KNOW BEFORE
# THE REAL FIGHT BEGINS

It was easier carrying my father's body to his grave years ago than engaging in a contested divorce and solicitation of physical custody of my children. His burial was natural and expected and followed the appointment of all men. In many conversations throughout our lives, death is discussed, and our mortality and that of others are dealt with. There is sadness with death, but not generally a lasting effect. Not so with divorce. For me, this was worse than anything I've had to endure. In the meantime, let me list some must-know(s) to help you work with a divorce and child custody issues. It is not an all-inclusive listing, but a good foundation for consideration.

Number one, *qualified therapeutic counseling should be considered.* The day my spouse began to move items from the home is the day counseling began for me (although it was supposed to be for both of us, as discussed). The Department of Veteran Affairs did the referral for the chosen therapist, which served as an unbiased approach for selection. A good counselor can adjust to changing situations that can help you individually and may later potentially serve as an expert witness to uncover truths. A good counselor can help you cope with major life-altering events. I would not write off faith-based counselors; however, experience showed conflicts whereby beliefs conflicted with the availability of court testimony.

Number two, a contested divorce can be expensive. Monies may be unavailable if it's part of the contested divorce assets. Don't expect the spouse to cooperate in the attainment of you getting access to accounts and other means of financing the divorce and custody process. *Your resources drive everything!* Lawyers don't work for free (in 99.9 percent of cases). Assess your financial situation as related to your employment, access to cash on hand, investments, ability to create another stream of income, home equity (if you're the sole owner), selling of items not essential, and even getting help from family and friends. As for the latter, I was fortunate to have individuals who were willing to help me finance the divorce and custody litigation throughout to keep me financially solvent. Asking for help is not a sign of weakness; it's a recognition that you can't do it alone, financially. You can replace items and money, but in the moment, financial support is a must. The longer you put off litigation to gather finances, the longer you may inadvertently have the delay work against you in the long run.

Number three, *you must quickly come to terms with the fact that family, coworkers, and other social relationships will change.* Some will choose to disassociate from you permanently or until an outcome is revealed. During your litigation, strong personal unknown beliefs may be expressed and not necessarily in your favor. Examples of such were an in-law who threatened my life, close relatives who vehemently expressed that children should be with the mother regardless, folk in social and religious circles who shunned me…If you view your decision for a contested divorce and attainment of primary child custody as warranted, you've got to know that your circle of relationships may become much smaller, and you'll feel alone at times. It may become essential to build a new set of associates in the middle of chaos. But don't walk this chaos alone!

Number four, *don't let your emotions get the best of you*! Divorce and custody issues are extremely emotional. Most likely the very worst of you and your estranged spouse will bubble to the surface. Both written and oral communications between my now-divorced and then-estranged spouse, coupled with the children having to communicate within a new reality, were not always beneficial. At some point, you must analytically work on the divorce and custody issues for your own sanity. Don't emote negatively (all the time). Be truthful. Look at the situation for its reality and wishful thinking. You should work to develop situations to evoke truth by recalling past events and appropriately working in the present to explain your defense. Take care of yourself physically, emotionally, psychologically, and spiritually. If you don't, who will? At the end of the day, even the best of listeners won't be able to give you unlimited, undivided attention. You've got to be prepared to "stand alone" for a period and fight the good fight. Yet ensure you don't lose your humanity.

Number five, *choose your attorneys wisely, and don't expect them to do everything for you.* You should be very proactive with the things you can do yourself, thus providing valuable information to your attorney in your case. Replace as needed up to and including rehiring an attorney. *Attorney number one* was terminated because he began to misrepresent my interest by working to settle against my stated interest to him. In a hearing, he leaned toward me, stating he's done this thing a thousand times and to trust him. His spoken words were that I should simply divorce and provide child support in that I would be better off going forward. The attorney who replaced him was exceptional. He fought for my interest, which led to the Chancery Court ultimately ruling in my favor. He represented me during the appellate courts, ultimately getting a favorable judgment out of the Supreme Court. Yet *attorney number two* was replaced when I appeared in Youth Court with *attorney number three* whose skills were acutely tailored to bring out several key truths under oath while providing advisement on child issues broached. *Attorney number two* was rehired to complete actions in the Mississippi appellate courts, which upheld my favorable Chancery Court decision, allowing *attorney number four* to skillfully work terms for my divorce on the grounds of "irreconcilable differences" (ironically) and is now skillfully working on my custody litigation. The point is that "you" must ensure your interests are being accurately represented with the right experience for the right court situation.

Number six, for child custody and pretrial issues up to and including working out visitation, guardians ad litem (GAL) (who are attorneys) may be appointed by courts to provide feedback to the court. They are assigned advocates for minors. View GALs as I described (in part) in the previous paragraph. *You have a say on the GAL selection.* The Youth Court experience will be addressed, but it became necessary to have a GAL removed for inappropriate and biased concerns recorded by me.

Number seven, *prepare yourself for court hearings, decisions, and opinions not favorable to your cause*. Also know that courts can rule against you in spite of your presentation of confirmed facts that a reasonable outsider would rule in your favor. Don't expect some judges to follow their own advisement from one hearing to the other. Courts have personalities that are set by the judge (or judges) overseeing the litigation of which the only baseline is not always the law. Yet the court's interpretation of a law may vary, needing correction by way of an appeal or other action. Depending on the case, the court process can be cumbersome and, in the case of some litigants, a tool to deliberately delay or create another jurisdictional situation (even out of state) or some other ploy to slow down or throw out your petitions altogether.

Number eight, *challenge the status quo outside of court working multiple fronts simultaneously*. The fight to attain truth went as far as me appealing to the Mississippi Attorney General's Office as related to my complaint of gender discrimination against Child Protective Services. As related to my complaint of gender discrimination with one judge, I filed a complaint with the Mississippi Judicial Review Board several times. In both cases, both entities in essence did not actively do anything except one very vital point; they were forced to give opinions that assisted me in making qualitative decisions on how to approach a judge with my grievances. Information empowers you to force a response to issues and concerns, which encourages "the system" to know you are serious. When you articulate concerns officially in writing, a response is warranted, and this forces entities to do so. Such actions don't even require attorney support or payment of services.

Number nine, *do not expect litigation to be speedy*. Don't expect the opposing party (or you) to be cooperative in the legal process. With contestation, expect numerous continuances, lengthy hearings, appeals not related to issues of law, and other legal distractions. Look at court as a potential legal brawl, a fight in which wounds will be on full display and made public (in most cases, minus those related to sensitive child issues), but low blows to make you falter.

Number ten, *communicate effectively always.* Anything you say, write, email, or put on social media can be used either for or against you even decades before. Effective communication "listens well," coupled with relaying information effectively. Never take conversations as isolated moments. They are extensions of a continuum that can be beneficial or harmful. A single conversation may very well be a puzzle piece that exposes the truth you need to defend your case or harm it. Yet I can't overemphasize; anything you say, write, or communicate to another can be used against you under oath!

# Warren County Chancery #2017-278GN

As a result of me not accepting a divorce initially on the grounds of "irreconcilable differences" along with the suggested terms of child custody, child support, division of property, and others, the test of my resolve began in honest January 2018. Of the several grounds of divorce that Mississippi acknowledges, my estranged spouse charged me with "habitual cruel and inhuman treatment" as her reasoning for solicitation of divorce since I would not agree to "irreconcilable differences." As defined by Mississippi law, my estranged spouse charged me with alleged conduct that endangered her life, limbs, and health or created a reasonable apprehension of such danger. In my case, I surmised that this charge was a form of "blackmail" to keep me from going to court. Her calculus was that I would not face the public spectacle of my life being laid bare with all its faults and somehow I would relent to all her demands for divorce and custody. My life and faults in fact were laid bare as well as hers; however, nothing proved her alleged grounds of divorce as noted in the final Chancery Court judgment in December 2018:

*IT IS, THEREFORE, ORDERED AND ADJUDGED: 1. That…Rankin's Complaint for Divorce on the ground of habitual cruel and inhuman*

*treatment is hereby denied. 2. That...Rankin's request*
*for attorney's fees and court costs is hereby denied. 3.*
*That in light of the ruling in this case, all other issues*
*in the Complaint for Divorce are hereby moot.*

Upon receipt of the judgment, my estranged spouse appealed to the Court of Appeals. The Chancery Court's judgment meant we were still married and custody issues concerning the children would be left unresolved (the latter creating issues of scheduled visitation and parental flight). The entirety of the year to reach the court's decision was filled with several hearings whereby conditions were being created by my spouse to entrap me to create a false narrative of spousal abuse and child neglect.

One notable hearing is related to a dance recital with my children. In lieu of communicating needed information with me, she simply ignored my physical presence and afterward attempted to create a public spectacle attempting to portray me as hostile; her only witness to such testimony was a colleague of hers among approximately three hundred persons in attendance for the recital. Second is Father's Day. After grilling a full meal, my younger child wanted hot dogs. Upon leaving the home to get hot dogs for my children (two minutes to the local convenience store), the younger triggered the alarm by going out the side door to the playhouse in an enclosed yard to retrieve a toy. She called her mother because at this juncture the children did not differentiate the responsibilities between the two of us. All was well; however, an act that had taken place over the entirety of the children's lives by both of us going to the store and leaving the children alone was being used as a reason for neglect...hypocritical standard. Neither issue gained traction in court.

This experience in the first of six courts did not challenge my interpretation of the legal process in that all seemed balanced, not biased toward my gender, but just a straightforward presentation and judgment based on facts presented. When a legitimate complaint does not exist against you, understand that the opposition may conjure up anything to create a situation to enhance unsubstantiated claims. Stand firm on truth. Don't lie under oath. The truth is an absolute defense. Engage the opposition accordingly.

# Warren County Youth Court Summons #19-062

*W*arning: This is the longest single read within this book but essential for showing its unintended benefits. From my observations, the Warren County Youth Court was not a "justice is blind" court. However, its involvement indirectly allowed time for issues to be discovered, which would be a foundation for eventually getting my divorce and a counter for the now-ensuring custody battle. It helped to develop situations and identify hidden incidents that were unknown to me in Chancery Court. The unknown would be answers I needed to our saga including reasons (in part) for my spouse's divorce petition. Youth Court cannot issue a divorce, but concerns broached in this court assisted me in the final attainment of my divorce under conditions I could accept.

On the very first day of Youth Court, decisions were made in favor of the mother even before evidence was presented. This court shields itself by having a preprinted statement on display and restated by the judge that testimony in Youth Court is not to be shared outside the courtroom. However, it does not preclude me from sharing orders issued, motions, or information I attained independently on my own. At my own peril, I will state upfront that the judge, without testimony being heard within minutes of the very first court hearing, emphatically emphasized that the mother would have temporary legal custody of the children. Yet the visitation plan mirrored that of Chancery Court before its final decision, which was two weeks on and off pending further hearings. As I walked out of the courtroom, my attorney quickly stated to me that if I wanted him to explain what had just happened, he could not. Even Chancery Court (a higher court) had not imposed such parental custody directives.

How did this case end up in Youth Court, which had no jurisdiction as noted in a later motion filed by my attorney, which legally laid out this fact? In a word, *deception*.

> *Through counsel, and files this his Motion to Dismiss showing unto the Court that in it's bench opinion of June 17, 2019, (order not yet entered) this Court as a matter of fact stated and found on record that the Court, even as of June 17, 2019, did not find any abuse and/or neglect in this matter, and this being the case this Court lacks jurisdiction of the parties and subject matter. WHEREFORE PREMISES CONSIDERED, Kelvin M. Rankin moves for entry of this Court's order dismissing this matter for lack of jurisdiction.*

What did my estranged spouse do to get Youth Court involved before my motion was filed for lack of jurisdiction? Approximately one month prior to the first Youth Court hearing, my elder daughter awakened me in the middle of the night. She told me that if I wanted to see her or her sibling again, I needed to stop "mama" from taking them to Georgia. After failing to attain a divorce in Chancery Court, seemingly my estranged spouse was going to execute parental flight, effectively preventing me from seeing the children while under the protection of Georgia jurisdiction. With no order in place, the move would have been legal with her establishing another legal residence with eventual jurisdiction as long as she could meet Georgia residency requirements. Between the decision rendered by Chancery Court and the need to immediately file for divorce and get her served to keep jurisdiction in Mississippi, she had to be delayed from her action of parental flight. Confirming this alleged flight plan was my daughter showing things on the computer up to and including the school her mother had picked out along with a dance studio. Immediately, I filed for divorce in part to keep jurisdiction in Mississippi. The petition in Youth Court would have had no powers to keep jurisdiction in Mississippi, especially with no subject matter of abuse and neglect present.

A must! My estranged spouse had to be served the divorce petition to keep the case in Mississippi. About three weeks after filing for divorce, she was served, and within the same hour, I, too, was served, with a summons to appear before Youth Court. To keep the girls in Mississippi prior to being served, there were days I kept them out of school to prevent her from immediately moving to Georgia. The children's school was the one place she could simply pick them up and depart. I even allowed one girl to go to school while I kept the other with me, surmising that she wouldn't leave with just one child. My actions were perfectly legal as long as I did not violate any state laws such as truancy (a set number of days absent without an excuse from school). Her petition before Youth Court was abuse and neglect of the children, which was determined to be baseless (at the time).

In that first Youth Court hearing, my estranged wife's attorney paraded my children's principal and the school's front desk secretary, whom I thought I had a good parental relationship with, along with the truancy officer, to provide testimony against me. Again the jurisdiction of Youth Court in my case was to review abuse and neglect. The review was found to be without merit as stated earlier. Of special concern was the truancy officer (a state law enforcement officer), who was given notes of my concern from the outset, noting my allegations of potential parental flight. In part below is an excerpt from that correspondence:

> *There is still concern of parental flight by…with the children to a location outside of the VWSD's oversight as well as mine. Yet, in keeping with the State of Mississippi's child attendance laws and applicable*

*policies within the VWSD I will be compliant with their attendance. The inability by you (your office) and me (coupled with my legal representative) to get and/or pursue a youth court hearing to address the issues of both school attendance and potential parental flight risk are duly noted. Therefore, other slower judicial means are being actively pursued. Per our conversation…historical recorded attendance has been exceptional except for the days with requested excused absences with corresponding events (coupled with my parental concerns during the month of February 2019).*

The above-addressed concerns broached to the principal, the secretary, and the truancy officer were not the focus of the opposing party. All automatically sided with the mother. No mention of my active participation with my children in school by the principal, the truancy officer *never* having grounds for her claims as a law enforcement officer for the state, nor the secretary stating the very active presence of me walking my children right up to the door entrance routinely.

During the first hearing, I got one very important thing from the judge, which was the children were to remain in the state of Mississippi (so I thought). Later when I discovered that my estranged spouse had moved to Georgia, I petitioned the court for temporary custody, having gotten guidance from the court that the children were to stay in Mississippi. To my surprise, the following was *a decision which was not petitioned by my estranged spouse*:

*A Review Hearing was held in regards to Custody and Placement wherein the children were to remain in the custody of…(mother); that the mother and father are to alternate vistiation with the children every two weeks until such time the 2019–2020 school term begins and at such time the minor children are to be in the physical custody of their mother*

*and to attend school in the school district in which*
*they live (State of Georgia).*

At that very moment, the children were taken away from me with the mother firmly in control of visitation. I never got to say goodbye. I did not get the residential address of my children. I was escorted out of Youth Court as if I were a criminal. I heard my children weeping in the other room. It was only later by way of my medical insurance that I was able to track down my children to a counselor in Georgia.

With the above decision, the Youth Court judge did not provide an adequate means of visitation. As often as I was allowed, I traveled to Georgia, which got very expensive. Both children were devastated at the ages of eight and ten. The mother assured the court she had adequate means to attend to the children's needs; however, this would later be discovered it was not the case. In March 2020, she reluctantly sent the children back to Mississippi because she was unemployed in part because of the COVID-19 pandemic of which she did not share those facts until an emergency hearing was invoked; the children gave enough indications that she was not working. I then refused to return the children pending a Youth Court hearing to determine the care and welfare of my children. My estranged spouse persuaded the Jefferson County Sheriff's Department (which had zero jurisdiction) to become involved, evoking the sheriff to issue an all-points bulletin to "Be on the Lookout" (BOLO) for me kidnapping the children. No AMBER alert was issued by the state's higher law enforcement agencies. More experienced law enforcement agencies in Claiborne and Warren Counties correctly directed my estranged spouse back to Youth Court.

Within eight hours of the BOLO, my face, vehicular tag number, pictures of my daughters, and last known locations were plastered on the local television station, Facebook, and various other outlets including radio. It was then that the court-appointed guardian ad litem reappointed himself by way of the court and called for an emergency hearing with the Youth Court judge. Personally I believe the court was in the dilemma of having to justify its previous decisions. I was not found in contempt of court, and the following was rendered in an order:

> *On 03/23/2020 the Court held review hearig on Motion of Guardian Ad Litem due to concerns GAL had in regards to the whereabouts of the minor children; all parties appearing teleconference; the father, Kelvin Rankin being represented by counsel,... The Court finding that the minor children had been going to school in...Georgia where her mother was living; that the father, Kelvin Rankin, was living in Warren County, Miss. at the marital domicile; that the children were in Warren County with their father. The Court finding that the minor children should be allowed to stay with their father for three weeks from this date; to return to their mother's physical custody for the next three week period; for the parents to each have a three week period of visitation with the children to be alternated every three weeks; that this Court retains jurisdiction until such time the parties seek an Order from this Court relinquishing jurisdiction for proceeding to be held in Chancery Court.*

Drastic change of events...*my children were back in my life on a consistent basis*! Because of COVID-19, they were in school remotely in Mississippi and doing well with their schooling along with being with me on a consistent basis. The development of a situation takes time and patience without knowing the end result. In this case, a bold action (not without risk of being charged with contempt of court) to not return the children proved beneficial. My concern was primarily for the children and not the letter of the law.

The estranged spouse had been ordered to place the children in counseling when they initially transferred to Georgia; however, she did not maintain that counseling. Therefore, on one of their visits, I began sending them to counseling with the Veteran Administration's family-recommended therapist. Both did well under her guidance, but it became evident that the mother was not pleased with the therapy. At one point during the rotational period, I was summoned on the charge of contempt for not returning the children a second time. I was found guilty of contempt of court and fined to pay my estranged wife's attorney (who was court-appointed for lack of finances) and court fees. One child had measurable high anxiety initiated by the actions of the mother, which were testified under oath by the therapist. Although I was fined in contempt of court and have this civil action on my record, I must confess that it was one of the best beneficial investments in this ordeal. The children were allowed by Youth Court to continue counseling with the therapist in person while in Mississippi and over videoconferences while in Georgia. Part of that September 2020 contempt order states:

> IT IS FURTHER ORDERED AND ADJUDGED *that KELVIN RANKIN (FATHER—BIOLOGICAL), is hereby ordered to pay…(PARENT REPRESENTATIVE FOR MOTHER) attorney fees;…GUARDIAN AD LITEM fees incurred due to the "willful contempt" of Kelvin Rankin from the date of the Petition for Contempt being filed through the date of the hearing on said contempt petition.*

Although fined, it was the only way to help my emotionally scarred child by way of evidence presented. The GAL assigned to the case was only interested in the letter of the order and not the interest of my children. It was probably at this hearing that I perceived that his interest shifted overwhelmingly to becoming *"pro-mom"* as I articulated to him in an email and verbally outside court. It was evident when he pretended never to have known the phrase.

In February 2021, I am amid a severe snowstorm, unable to travel, and trapped in my home. Thankfully, I am unable to travel. During this storm, one of my children revealed hidden truths that would succinctly explain everything related to the initial divorce petition and child custody. Yet once again when the children were returned to my care, I definitively refused to send them back to their mother until a hearing was held for a third time. Dark secrets were revealed during a videoconference and confirmed once they returned for a face-to-face with the therapist. If I had been found in contempt of court, I was prepared to appeal unlike during the much earlier request on my "motion to dismiss" because of this court's lack of jurisdiction. This court was finally faced with legitimate abuse and neglect charges but could not act as noted in parts:

> *Present for the hearing was…(Special Appointed Youth Court Prosecutor),…(Attorney for Father),… (Attorney for Mother),…(Guardian Ad Litem)… (MDCPS case worker)…(Mother—Biological) and Kelvin Rankin (Father—Biological) in attendance before this Court.*

> *IT IS FURTHER, ORDERED that the Court is without jurisdiction as to the issue of the allegation…having occurred outside the jurisdiction of this Court; therefore, the petition in regards to the allegation…should be and is hereby dismissed for lack of jurisdiction;…*

> *IT IS FURTHER, ORDERED that…motion to find Kelvin Rankin in Contempt of Court for failure to timely return the minor children to… Rankin as ordered by this Court should be and is hereby dismissed.*

Although this court found itself inadequate and without legitimate subject matter to adjudicate the initial presentation, when faced with a real criterion for which Youth Court exists, no real admonishment was targeted toward the mother. Outside court, I took measures to actively demonstrate that the judge was not simply biased but discriminatory toward me based on gender of which an appeal was recommended as an option. The judge assumed that jurisdiction would quickly transfer to Chancery Court to take the case while the estranged wife was awaiting her Court of Appeals decision. My gut feeling is that the judge was attempting to assist the mother with the ensuing custody hearings to be had in Chancery Court.

Youth Court from one perspective exercised legal incompetence (from my perspective). However, situations were revealed due to its acceptance of unsubstantiated subject matter in the beginning. After over two years, the final order from Youth Court was the allowance of minor children to make decisions where they wanted to reside with the knowledge of damning evidence. No higher court in Mississippi, to my knowledge, exercises such authority of allowing children alone to make decisions. It's at the age of twelve that children can state their preference, and one child had not met that threshold. Higher courts only use it as a basis for the whole of the decision (Albright Factors). Youth Court ended with parts of the following:

> *Having considered the testimony of the parties, the arguments of their counsel, the statements and wishes of the minor children—which was based on good reasoning and rationale—and the testimony and recommendation of the Guardian Ad Litem, and considering the best interests of the minor children.*

> *IT IS THEREFORE ORDERED AND ADJUDGED*

> 1. *That the minor child,…, shall reside with and be placed in the custody of her mother,…, where she will attend school in the State of Georgia, where she resides with her mother until further Order of the Court.*

> 2. *That the minor child,…shall reside with and be placed in the custody of her father, Kelvin Rankin, and attend school in the State of*

*Mississippi where she shall reside until further*
*Order of the Court.*

On the date of the above judgment, the children were legally separated from each other. One with me and one with the mother. The lingering question for all has been "What if the overwhelming evidence was against me, what would have been the outcome?" I wasn't the judge, but from my lay position, I can surmise that I believe the judge would have given both children to the mother. This is the same judge who awarded custody of both children to the mother at the onset. *What changed?* What changed is that in view of the facts (subjectively) in my favor, the judge was not going to give me custody of both children. My opinion is that she hid behind the protections of state law to exercise gender discrimination of which her judgments (most likely) in an appeal would have been overturned. However, knowing that the children had preferences as they had later began to articulate, I believe the court used this as a means to begin resolving itself of the "mess" it inappropriately assumed under its jurisdiction. An appeal early on would have only complicated a situation and cost more while the estranged spouse had the Chancery Court ruling before the Court of Appeals.

Now on to court number three of five as of January 2023, but not before mentioning the entities of Child Protective Services along with the guardian ad litem related to Youth Court.

# CHILD PROTECTIVE SERVICES (CPS) and GUARDIAN AD LITEM (GAL) (2019–2023)

## Warren County

Child Protective Services (CPS) and guardian ad litem (GALs) served as intermediaries to the Warren County Youth Court. Their input was only as valuable as the officiating judge deemed necessary and seemed to support a narrative that was antifather. Nothing of reasonable effect was ever declared negative against the mother (even with evidence presented by my counsel). Remember there was never any issue of neglect or abuse found against me; however, not so for the mother. After reviewing official notes attained at the conclusion of Youth Court, I discovered that the integrity of CPS is only as dependable as the integrity of the social worker preparing the written report summary. CPS was used by my estranged spouse numerous times of which each incident was found to be without merit. In stark contrast to the two times I reported incidents to CPS, overwhelming evidence was provided, validated by the court-approved counselor, reviewed by an independent entity responsible to the court, and then presented before Youth Court. The undisclosed incidents in this book will not be mentioned. Faced with a dilemma of questionable jurisdiction from the outset but faced with real facts of credible abuse and neglect, Youth Court used "jurisdiction" as a legitimate excuse not to pursue the discovery made by me. In fact I did file my grievances in the jurisdiction of responsibility.

Although the Warren County Youth Court maintained jurisdiction and my allegation was found to be credible, I took the extra step of appealing CPS's findings to the Mississippi Attorney General's (AG's) office as it was in opposition to facts. On the incident in question, the CPS counselor and I clashed from the beginning as if I were already guilty. When one of my two daughters was questioned about the incident prior to my interaction with the social worker, she came crying to me, stating that the counselor did not believe her. The AG's office did grant me a hearing with the court-appointed therapist as my witness while CPS had the counselor's first-, second-, and third-line supervisors present for the videoconference (not under oath). All from CPS were women, no men. As a matter of fact, all decisions and interactions, including those with the legal advisor for CPS, were made by women. Men need representation in this agency.

Weeks afterward, I received the official findings recommended from the administrative hearing officer to the commissioner. In part, it read:

> *The evidence presented at this administrative hearing supports a finding that the claim…as defined by Miss Code. Ann…is unsubstantiated. The evidence presented also shows that, despite Rankin's Formal Grievances against MDCPS and…, no punitive action was warranted.*

And,

> *After hearing the evidence presented,…the MDCPS has established substantial evidence…This recommendation has no bearing on the investigation… in…Mississippi.*

A "*win*" is not always getting what you think is fair. Exposure is priceless. CPS is an entity that by itself does not and cannot make final decisions. Remember the recommendation to the commissioner was not under oath; it was not worth going further. But what I did get was the entire investigative report prepared by the CPS worker, which denoted bias (discrimination) by her. Because of ongoing custody issues, let me share this small part of the entire investigative report prepared by the CPS worker, of which she made this among other suggestions to thwart the truth discovered:

> *Suggested to…that she should find a different therapist for the girls…agreed and stated she wanted a different therapist.*

Also, the worker claimed I manipulated one child to misrepresent essential facts although all was found to be factual. I can only assume that at the children's time of need for counseling, part of the biased recommendation by the worker played into the court's decision to end therapy as ordered by the Youth Court. It is important to know you're fighting battles of which you'll lose some, but you need to win the war!

Guardians ad litem are lawyers. They're supposed to be representatives concerning the children's best interest, reporting findings and recommendations to the court (unbiasedly). One guardian ad litem was removed at the last hearing at my request as mentioned in the order. It was done without any extensive conversation in court. It was my observation that he seemed fair initially; however, I realized at some point he was "pro-mom" regardless of the facts presented. I then bombarded him with emails stating observations of mismanagement to which he never replied. Without fanfare or debate, the judge released him. It is my belief that conversations took place in which the GAL and the court realized that much would be exposed; silence or inaction is a response, and the GAL being removed quietly was an example of such. Special note, you have a say about a GAL's appointment. If you have issues before or during custody issues, broach the topic. GALs are given broad authority; however, they don't supersede a judge's intervention. As a matter of record, my request to remove the GAL was noted in the order:

> *IT IS FURTHER ORDERED AND ADJUDGED*
> *that the request by Kelvin Rankin for the Guardian*

*Ad Litem,…, Esq. to be removed as Guardian Ad Litem, is granted, and…, Esq. is hereby relieved of his duties as Guardian Ad Litem in this matter upon the conclusion of the hearing of this matter on August 2, 2021.*

# In the Court of Appeals of the State of Mississippi #2019-CA-00238-COA

After my then-estranged spouse failed to prove her case on the grounds of "habitual cruel and inhuman treatment" (Court #1: Chancery Court), she then filed a petition to the Court of Appeals (COA). *It is important to note that the appeal sought after by my spouse is 100 percent her version of how wrong the judged ruled in our initial case.* Within weeks of filing her appeal, she had me summoned to Youth Court (Court #2: Youth Court) on grounds of neglect, abuse, and truancy toward our minor children, creating over-lapping jurisdictions at the same time. Recall in Youth Court that my claim was that the spouse was attempting parental flight to Georgia to change jurisdiction that she assumed would be more favorable to her divorce and custody petitions. She's never denied this allegation by me when confronted by me. Both in Chancery and Youth Courts under oath, the mother vehemently denied she was moving to Georgia. Yet she established a successful foothold in Youth Court, giving her some coverage while simultaneously establishing a Georgia residence. Had I not gotten her served for my petition for divorce, she could have legally moved with the children to Georgia, established residency, effectively had the law on her side in denying me access to the children, and could have filed for divorce in Georgia's jurisdiction. Had she been successful, resources and hearings out-of-state would have probably caused me to concede to her demands.

Subjectively I do not believe the estranged spouse would have kept her petition before the COAs and that it was a ploy. If she had not been served with my divorce petition before Youth Court or had I not been tipped off of her plans of parental flight, nothing would have prevented her from residing in Georgia while then cancelling the appeal process filed in Mississippi. It was only after she was served with my divorce petition that jurisdiction was firmly established in Mississippi (not in the COA). Youth Court, being the lowest of the courts encountered, could only issue temporary orders in such matters as has been described. Chancery Court in Mississippi is the primary court that has the authority to render decisions concerning divorce and custody unless the appellate courts reverse and render (or remand) a decision over any other subordinate court.

For the audience at large, the Court of Appeals only reviews the material and testimony presented at trial in Chancery Court of which the divorce petition originated. They reviewed my case for errors and issued a thirteen-page decision. Honestly their decision shocked me! The majority rule opinion decided to "reverse and remand" the lower court's decision. In the majority opinion, they noted:

> *We find that…presented sufficient evidence, which if believed, established that Kelvin's behavior negatively affected her overall demeanor and caused her physical harm (e.g., migraines and elevated blood pressure). Accordingly, having determined that the chancery court erred in summarily concluding there was insufficient evidence of habitual cruel and inhuman treatment, we remand to the chancery court for further consideration in accordance with this opinion.*

The dissenting judges rightly articulated what I've known for years and what was testified by the estranged spouse under oath:

> *Asserts that the chancellor erred by not conducting a subjective inquiry into how Kelvin's conduct*

*affected her. But the record shows that the chancellor considered the evidence before her. Simply because the chancellor denied...request for a divorce does not mean she did not consider how Kelvin's conduct affected... Furthermore, while...testified that she suffered from migraines and elevated blood pressure when she lived with Kelvin, she testified that she was diagnosed with migraines in high school and that she was never diagnosed with high blood pressure. Therefore, unlike the majority, I cannot say that... established that Kelvin's behavior negatively affected her overall demeanor and caused her physical harm.*

Some of the evidence cited for the majority opinion really surprised me as being the reasoning for their decision. It was as if the majority opinion and the dissenting opinion were looking at two different cases. The only direct quote from my estranged spouse used by the majority in their opinion demonstrated (in my subjective opinion) a prejudicial rebuke against me as a Veteran and those who have or are serving. If there was ever an example of the concerns broached by those who serve or have served in the Armed Forces about how courts may negatively view them, this as part of their reasoning brokers that concern:

*[H]is harm to me has always been emotionally, mentally, and spiritually...As he testified, he was an army ranger, he was an instructor and army ranger. That is what he specialized in, in mental abuse. And that is what he did. So, the physical abuse, I probably could have handled that ten times better than the mental abuse that I had to suffer at his hands for those ten years I stayed in the home with him.*

Firstly, I was a qualified Ranger and served at a Ranger Training Company as one of a select group of seasoned "second- and third-time" company grade commanders. Secondly, I was not a Ranger instructor. There were Ranger instructors under my command of whom I ensured the safe and effective training environment was provided to ensure (in part) that dignity and respect were protected. Thirdly, my estranged spouse's testimony in Chancery or any other venue has never broached a cause of mental or physical abuse based on what I did at the Ranger Training Battalion at that time thirteen years prior and before we were married. No doubt, Ranger School is still considered the toughest leadership school in the Army, but I can assuredly state that my estranged spouse or the justices were not qualified to use this as a means of reasoning. It was a slap in the face to me and Veterans who've served in such positions. When you don't have a case, grasping for straws is the norm.

Next steps, the dismissed attorney (attorney number two), who counterfiled on my behalf to the Court of Appeals, called me up. He was convinced we could win "on writ of certiorari," which I'll explain in the next chapter. Look at it as an appeal for now. But that attorney was an exceptionally talented lawyer. He laid out my courses of action: *Option 1*: We go back to Chancery Court under the advisement of the opinion (reversed and remanded) which would go back before the same judge for reconsideration. This option could have resulted in yet another appeal on the same case or a reversal of my previous favorable decision. *Option 2*: Negotiate terms for a divorce on irreconcilable differences with a COA opinion that would be the final say about my character leaving questions. Option 3: Appeal the decision to the Supreme Court of Mississippi in an attempt to "reinstate and affirm" the original decision of the Chancery Court, rendering the Court of Appeals majority decision moot. I chose to "carry on" to the Supreme Court with *Option* 3.

At this juncture, I was in two courts (Youth Court and Court of Appeals), moving to the Supreme Court with a hopeful outcome that would remove my spouse's delaying tactics and would then have my divorce petition heard in Chancery Court. Until the appeal process was complete, I would remain married, and the custody issues would not be heard before a Chancery Court until the resolution of "habitual cruel and inhuman treatment" was resolved.

# In the Supreme Court
# of Mississippi
# #2019-CT-00238-SCT

Most Mississippi divorces end as "irreconcilable differences," with appearances in Chancery Courts and appeals to the appellate court(s) being less frequent. "Irreconcilable differences" simply is an agreed-upon divorce with possible issues like assets and even custody needing resolution, but in many cases, these issues are resolved between attorneys or the couple themselves. Contested divorces expose the nakedness of your life (lives) and become an easily accessible public record for *everyone* at the stroke of a key! The fate of my future and the final decision on my character were presented to the Mississippi Supreme Court.

Technically my Supreme Court case was reviewed under "on writ of certiorari." It was a matter of reviewing the decision of the lower court:

> *This certiorari case considers whether the Court of Appeals' decision is in conflict with a prior published decision of this Court. Because we find that the Court of Appeals' decision conflicts not only with a recently published decision of this Court but also with longstanding principles of appellate review, we*

> *reverse the decision of the Court of Appeals, and we reinstate and affirm the judgment of the chancery court.*

As part of the court's due diligence, it noted several cases that directed it to "reinstate and affirm" the original Chancery Court's decision, showing that my estranged spouse's complaint for divorce and other issues were moot. The irony is that *attorney number two* was an attorney for what was then the most recent case concerning what constituted "habitual cruel and inhuman treatment" under the law. That case was Wangler *v.* Wangler; therefore, my attorney was acutely aware of the subject matter, which allowed him to present the facts under the law. As with the prestated case, Rankin *v.* Rankin was a majority decision. As in the Court of Appeals, it appeared that the two viewpoints of the majority and dissenting judges were interpreting the laws and evidence very differently. For the majority, one of many notes within the order states:

> *Despite this longstanding principle of appellate review, the Court of Appeals failed to recognize the required assumption "that the chancellor resolved [the credibility] issue[] in favor of [Kelvin]." Id. (citing Marascalco, 445 So. 2d at 1380). We agree with Kelvin that the Court of Appeals' decision conflicts with this Court's prior decision in Wangler. Indeed, Wangler, as well as the principles of appellate review discussed above, undermine the Court of Appeals' decision.*

I am a resident of the state of Mississippi and, therefore, under its laws. The Mississippi Supreme Court's majority rule maintained the standard of review that restored my credibility. Had this fight not been fought, I assure you that I would have felt as if I were a second-class citizen without absolution. To have reached this point affected me in the most negative of ways—my health, my mind, my career advancements, addition of debt, and other things—but to reach this decision was well worth the effort. *Rankin* v. *Rankin* is now a case law that has and will continue to help men as related to unfounded accusations of "habitual cruel and inhuman treatment" in part based on my personal observation of gender bias/discrimination.

In stark contrast, the dissenting judges had many comments. From my observations, their interpretation of the law was being rewritten into another context. As I stated with the Court of Appeals, the appellate courts can only use what was presented in the original case in Chancery Court (Court #1). For the record, I attest that all testimony from my estranged spouse was not as I recalled it to be factually based. Even the dissenting judges noted I gave truthful testimony that was the most embarrassing. But as my attorney in Chancery Court advised me, "*Don't lie under oath!*"

Below is an excerpt from the dissenting judges showing (in part) a reason they would have reversed and remanded the lower court's decision in favor of my estranged spouse:

> *The next day, . . . Rankin was awakened by the sound of a truck coming up the driveway. She feared that her husband had come back to hurt her. She testified that it was during this state of fear that she realized she had to leave, "because the feeling was so real that [she], honestly, thought that he had come back to hurt 17 [her]." This incident illustrates that, at the very least, Kelvin Rankin's pattern of emotional and verbal abuse had created in the mind of . . . Rankin a reasonable apprehension of danger to her life, limb, or health.*

I am not sure if the dissenting judges are psychologists, but it surely seemed that they took the liberty to make assertions as to the mind of my estranged spouse. What the judges failed to note is that with years of marital counseling, there was never (*not one*) any allegation of spousal abuse, no police reports, no credible witnesses, and not even her own testimony prior to their review. I cannot state for surety if they were aware of this aspect of my marriage. What I had sadly was a very dysfunctional marriage devoid of "habitual cruel and inhuman treatment." In a similar fashion, the same judges who dissented in the *Wangler* v. *Wangler* decision were the same in opposition to the majority opinion of *Rankin* v. *Rankin*. The Chancery Court judge who issued the original decision noted my marriage against the claim of "habitual cruel and inhuman treatment" succinctly as such:

> *A marriage may become unpleasant and argumentative, but not rise to the level of being so unnatural and infamous as to warrant the grant of divorce on the ground of habitual cruel and inhuman treatment. Killen v. Killen, 54 So.3d 869, 873 (~14) (Miss.Ct.App.2010). Les and Lonnie may have an unhappy and incompatible marriage, but Lonnie has failed to prove that Les's behavior rises to the level of habitual cruel and inhuman treatment.*

A date and judgment that is part of my life story—"*Thursday, 12th day of August, 2021 The Judgment of the Court of Appeals is Reversed. The Judgment of the Warren County Chancery Court is Reinstated and Affirmed.*" With this decision, I could now move forward to attain a divorce without "habitual cruel and inhuman treatment" being used as a blackmailing tool. Additionally, I could take keynotes back to Chancery Court (from Youth Court) to show my real value as a father, contrasting what were attempts at creating a false narrative of an abusive and neglectful father.

# Warren County Chancery #2019-037-GN

Now with the opinion given by the Supreme Court on a "writ of certiorari" affirming the lower court's decision that my estranged spouse's petition for divorce was moot, I could begin to fully engage my petition of divorce and custody matters in Chancery Court filed February 14, 2019. My petition as the plaintiff was recorded (in part) as:

> *That Plaintiff has endeavored to be a good, faithful and loving husband unto Defendant but that Defendant has been guilty of desertion for a continuous period in excess of one (1) year, habitual cruel and inhuman treatment of Plaintiff or, in the alternative, that the marriage of the parties met with irreconcilable differences all as such would entitle Plaintiff unto a divorce absolute of and from Defendant.*

> *Plaintiff, therefore, moves the Court for an Order of this Court awarding him the following: Temporary care, control and custody of the minor children of the parties, pending a final hearing in this cause*

> *with Defendant to be granted reasonable temporary*
> *visitation of the minor children that will not inter-*
> *fere with the best interest and welfare of said minor*
> *children.*

We settled for divorce on grounds of "irreconcilable differences" on June 16, 2022, and for me, half the fight had concluded, restoring my integrity as needed. I would not be known for having committed "habitual cruel and inhuman treatment" as was her alleged ground for divorce. I refused to have that ground used as a blackmailing tool to "scare" me into submitting to terms of divorce that I could not agree upon, without a full disclosure which required a trial. The main ensuing fight yet to be heard before the Chancey Court is my petition for permanent physical custody of my children. Between August 21, 2022, and the final date of our divorce decree, out-of-court conversations were taking place between attorneys to come to an out-of-court decision. During a Youth Court hearing, attorney number three did an excellent job exposing facts that if they had been known would have been broached in the very first Chancery Court hearing. However, in trying to broker a divorce settlement, attorney number three's tactics were akin to giving more concessions even with the decision coming out of the Supreme Court in my favor. Attorney number four stepped in and, in a very short order, brokered the divorce with everything to be settled before the Chancery Court judge.

Youth Court (having found no neglect or abuse by me, however lacking jurisdiction against my now divorced wife) was an unintended battleground that added additional evidence to the one and only hearing held in the ongoing Chancery Court under another judge. A continuance is in effect until another date is identified to potentially resume our custody hearing. *This book in fact will need a sequel.* Therefore, as related to what took place in the first hearing in January 2023, it will be wise for me not to delve into any details except that the best thing being in Chancery Court is that Youth Court truly is *done* exerting any authority. I'm simply grateful for the unintended consequences of attaining knowledge I did not know.

# TOP EIGHT PUBLIC/
# PRIVATE ATTACKS

Let me summarize in greater detail select points as personalized attacks instigated by my estranged spouse along with others. Again the truth is an absolute truth, and when all else fails, the opposition will resort to lies and deceit. These are actual incidents and misleading characterizations that in some cases elicited endangerment to my life and my children or attempts to portray my character as less than ideal, with no particular order of mentioning. Just understand that in my case, the kitchen sink and everything else were thrown at me. This is not an all-inclusive list, just highlights appropriate to the articulation of what I faced.

Number one: probably the most inappropriate zealous action of the Jefferson County Sheriff's Department was allowing my then-estranged spouse to issue a "Be on the Lookout (BOLO)" for kidnapping my children. This law enforcement agency did not have jurisdiction, nor had I lived in Jefferson County since 1988 as my wife had claimed. The sheriff's department (without any fact-finding) alerted several television and news outlets, which caused my daughters' immense fear that followed days after the sheriff's inaptitude. Many encouraged me to sue the department, but that would have been another item; to deal with that would have taken immense time away from my divorce and custody proceedings. Attorney number three at the time supposedly issued a cease and desist order preventing the sheriff's office from taking further action. When the facts were presented, the social media post that the sheriff's department had on their Facebook site suddenly disappeared without ever being seen again. When I personally confronted the local television station that had run the sheriff's unfounded allegations and that they could be sued, they immediately blamed the sheriff's office for their information as being supposedly trustworthy and stopped airing the alleged incident. Probably the worst things of all were the heavily armed sheriff along with his deputies who went to the wrong home of which I had resided years earlier. The now ex-wife lied to him, and no actions were taken against her. This incident mentioned in an earlier chapter is where the children were voluntarily given to me because she was unemployed and needed me to care for them. It was reported to me that my estranged spouse tried to get two other county sheriff's departments involved, but they declined because of jurisdiction and advised her to seek resolution in Youth Court. Imagine the world we live in today; a vigilante could have harmed my daughters in a quest to capture or kill me. The Jefferson County Sheriff's Department Facebook page read (in part) as such with the heading of KIDNAPPING BOLO:

> *BE ON THE LOOKOUT FOR 49 YEAR OLD KELVIN MAURICE RANKIN, THE FATHER OF 10 YEAR OLD…AND…MR. RANKIN WAS SUPPOSE TO RETURN THE GIRLS TO THEIR MOTHER,…BUT FAILED TO RETURN THE CHILDREN. MR. RANKIN IS BELIEVED TO BE TRAVELING IN A 2017 BLACK DODGE RAM 1500 PICKUP/MS TAG: KMR1. THE KNOWN HOMES (JEFFERSON COUNTY AND WARREN COUNTY) OF MR. RANKIN WERE CHECKED AND MR. RANKIN AND THE GIRLS WERE NOT AT EITHER LOCATION. IT IS UNKNOWN WHAT DIRECTION OF TRAVEL HE IS HEADED.*

This was the incident that broached a Youth Court emergency hearing that allowed my children to be reunited with me following a modified court order providing definitive visitation on a regular rotational basis during the COVID-19 epidemic. I was not charged with kidnapping. In my opinion, the county's leading law enforcement officer exercised negligence. But it's important for the reader to know (in my opinion) that men in custody cases are (moreover) considered guilty until innocence is proven.

Number two: at the release of the Supreme Court's decision, bloggers used excerpts to entertain their followers by providing commentary on content that evoked strong opinions that were misleading. A Twitter user out of California who identifies himself under the title of "*litigator, attorney, appeals, entertainment*" made the following comment to initiate a Twitter strand with strong alarming concerns. The Twitter blogger initiated the conversation this way but added much more to instigate the conversation:

> *Things I bet you didn't know existed in 2021: the Mississippi Supreme Court DENIES a woman a divorce because her evidentiary showing didn't constitute "habitual cruel and inhuman treatment... Trigger warning, as I am about to quote some of the stuff that the Mississippi Supreme Court held was insufficient to justify a divorce decree.*

Replies below were some of the tamer comments. As of the date I downloaded this elongated tweet, not one statement was objective. The decision out of the Supreme Court grew comments that were more political than factual to the case for this blogger and followers:

1. *"Sounds like Kelvin might meet with an 'accident' in the near future."*
2. *"For all you so called Christians in Mississippi, the statutes are eerily similar to Sharia Law."*
3. *"They won't let women get abortions this is just an extension of that. This is sickening."*
4. *"Mississippi has long been a proponent of treating some humans as property to be owned, ruled, managed, controlled."*
5. *"I mean, it's Mississippi. Can't she just shoot him?"*

6.  *"Let me guess, judge is a man a rethiglican and conservative hypocrite. Mississippi is some 4rd s******* country."*

My undergraduate degree was in English Communication, and the one thing I learned is that context matters. Several other bloggers followed suit in feeding their followers with a biased yet unbalanced perspective. Reminiscent of one deciding if they are going to watch their favorite news leaning of liberal or conservative, this is dangerous—not just for folk who would do me harm, but in the public domain of hopeful civil debate.

Number three: one of my former in-laws whom I knew many years before meeting my wife threatened my life! As facts began to become uncovered over time, it was evident (in my opinion) that not accepting a mutually agreed-upon divorce was the right answer. Through all the courts, it was *time, patience, and long-suffering* that revealed the truth and would be most beneficial to my children. Truth hurts, but at the core, it's an absolute defense. What was revealed was also a shocker to him, but the in-law refused to face the facts. Over a forty-five-minute telephonic rant from the individual, I informed them they were being recorded; they didn't care. They accused me of lies, although the issues were eventually noted during a lower court hearing; I had already filed a report with the Warren County Sheriff's Department of being threatened with bodily harm. Sadly emotions can run high, and for the record, situations concerning divorce and custody require levelheadedness and awareness of potential scenarios to ensure you do all you can do to de-escalate a situation.

Number four: in the follow-up to the initial hearing concerning the petition for divorce and temporary custody, my then-estranged spouse's attorney described my actions as being that of a pedophile. This ticked me off, and I responded as such not holding back my thoughts! From the very time my children were conceived to this very day, I've cared for them appropriately. At the time when the children were very young and in need of both direct and indirect supervision when taking a bath, my assistance at times was needed to help them with their understanding of how to care for themselves. I vehemently did not appreciate the insinuation. Her second attorney, who took over her defense later, tried to backtrack her first attorney's comments by stating the word *pedophile* was not used. The accusation was not seen as being received by the court very well. My aggressive comeback was that the description used was that of a pedophile, and by any other description, that is what it was, describing me as a pedophile. Men, defend your character. My subjective review of cases shows that this is a typical allegation that is sometimes used to force you to quit and succumb to the facade of "you can't win."

Number five: in an attempt to solicit false sympathy, she accused me of pet cruelty. I walked the dog more often than she did and took it for rides; when it was attacked by a neighbor's dog, I rushed it to the vet, incurring debt. In short, I cared for the dog more than her. However, anything about a pet by itself had absolutely nothing to do with my divorce or custody. For some pets are truly their family, but they're not blood relatives, and this statement can evoke serious feelings, which I do respect. An example of one social media comment of how such accusations can elicit strong emotions is a comment that stated: "*If a m*****f***** did that to my dog he wouldn't be needing a divorce he'd be needing a coffin.*" So if an opposing attorney believes they can subjectively appeal to the sensitivities of a judge about any such claim, they may well use such and any other tactics not steeped in fact but can attempt to get you to act out of character under oath, defending something that has nothing to do with the subject matter at hand.

Number six: adultery accusation…my former spouse accused me of having an affair with my former supervisor who later became a friend to both of us over the years. She cared for our children, ate at our table, went to church with us, and only showed the concern one would expect of a friend. My supervisor's daughter was even hired by my wife to work for her. Since being married in 2007, I affirm I never committed adultery, and absolutely no one else has accused me of such. Adultery is a ground for divorce in Mississippi. Had this lie been believed, it could have created a falsehood to be defended against.

Number seven: unfounded accusations that I was molested as a child, which is a lame attempt to grasp at straws concerning anything with my mentality. The reality is that I've never been abused in my youth or adulthood. I was "whooped," which was an upgraded spanking, yet it was always done as an appropriate disciplinary method by my parents, in school by principals and teachers, and as needed among family and very few others. Really could not wrap my brain around the tactic of using this accusation other than taking situations completely out of context to yet again create a false narrative.

Number eight: by no means is this the last of many false allegations thrown at me, but using the children as pawns simply hurts. They were placed in the middle of a fight, and their innocence was lost. There are no words to convey the tears and crying I witnessed they pour out. Children are not immune from this travesty. I swear before God that I never attempted to make the children choose sides, but their mom did. She at the onset stated that Daddy needed to learn a lesson. It was evident she thought (like so many) by default that she alone was owed custody. My children just wanted their parents, but with opposing views, one parent is more wrong than the other. Children adjust, but it takes away from who they are or will become later.

# THE SEQUEL YET TO
# BE WRITTEN

Patience is not the right word to use when engaging in such an elongated fight; long-suffering is more appropriate. A relationship as long as mine will and does have long-term impacts on many fronts beyond what was not obvious to me.

Sadly time is the one thing I or my children will ever get back as they are experiencing a loss of innocence as children. As of August 8, 2023, this entire ordeal has taken 2,071 days—1,653 days from the date my ex-wife filed for divorce until we got divorced, 1,433 days before my petition could be heard in this current Chancery Court, and 1,345 days from the date of the petition for divorce filed against me until the Supreme Court rendered its decision. All these overlapping benchmarks have taken over 5.67 years.

Now with the divorce behind us, temporary sole custody of one child, solicitation before Court #5 (Warren County Chancery Court #2019-037-GN) for the other, and my integrity proven to be whole, I know I've done everything as a man possible to prove my worth as a former husband and always a very active father.

My concern will be the following: regardless of the future decision of the present court, I must (1) be diligent to restore as much as possible my children's understanding of their identity, (2) establish for both children a sense of security as the one under my care presently experiences every day, and (3) work to gain some working civil relationship with the children's mother; there will be weddings (hopefully), grandchildren (hopefully), and many other celebrations along with challenges that will require our presence.

# ABOUT THE AUTHOR

Kelvin Rankin is a native of Lorman, Mississippi, and an Army veteran having been commissioned as an infantry officer in 1992. Rankin earned two master's degrees, which were in divinity (2009) from Wesley Biblical Seminary and a joint degree in workforce education leadership from Mississippi and Alcorn State Universities (2016). Rankin enjoys working the family farm, hunting, fishing, traveling, and occasionally doing public speaking. Kelvin is the father of two children currently twelve and fourteen.

www.ingramcontent.com/pod-product-compliance
Lightning Source LLC
Chambersburg PA
CBHW022121150726
47990CB00003B/1443